LOYISOMKIZEART

KWEZI™

COLLECTOR'S EDITION
ISSUE: 10 - 12

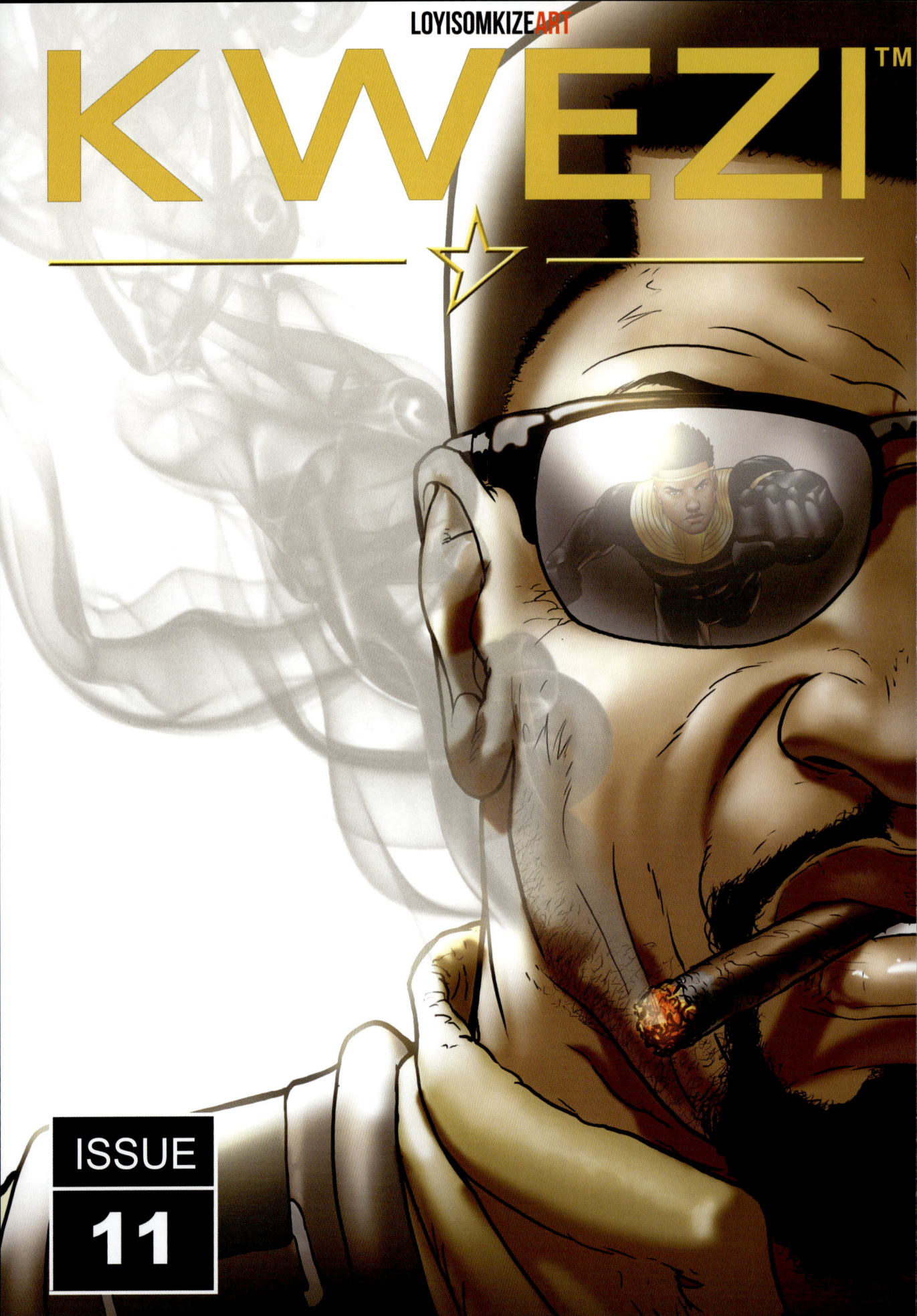

THIS IS NOTHING BUT A DISTRACTION! KHOI, WE NEED TO GET MAMADOU'S FAMILY! HE'S GOING TO RUN OUT OF OIL!

UNDERSTOOD.

DON'T WORRY, WE'LL GET YOU OUT AS SOON AS POSSIBLE. ALL OF YOU!

MAMADOU! I COULD REALLY USE A HAND OVER HERE!

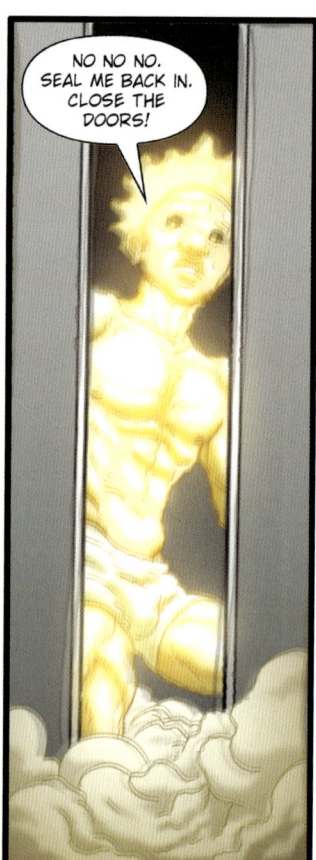

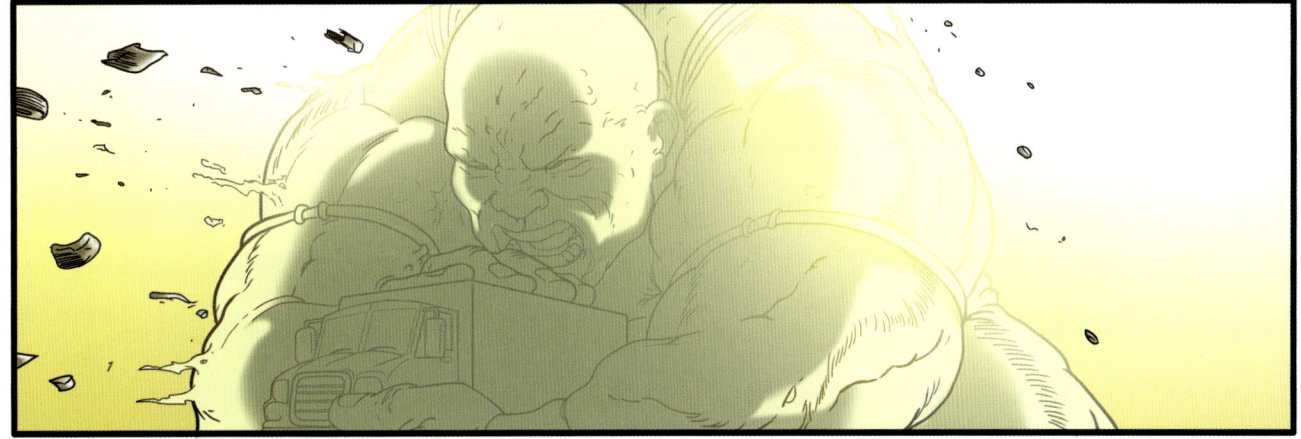

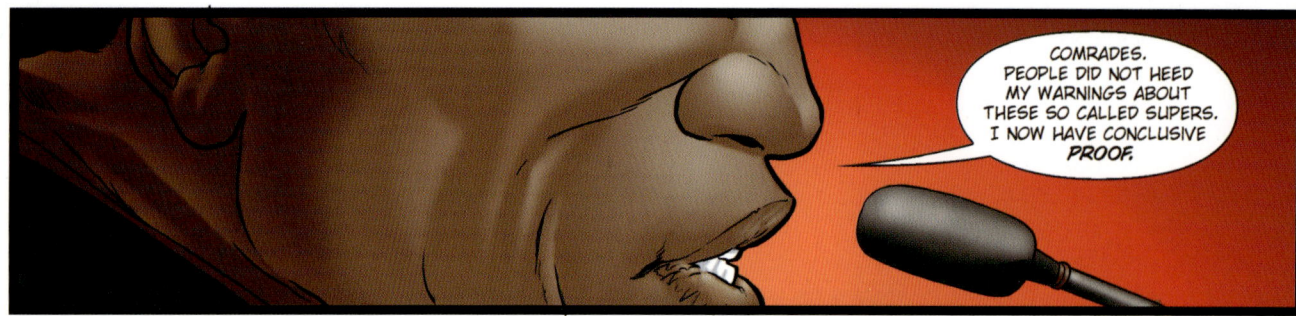

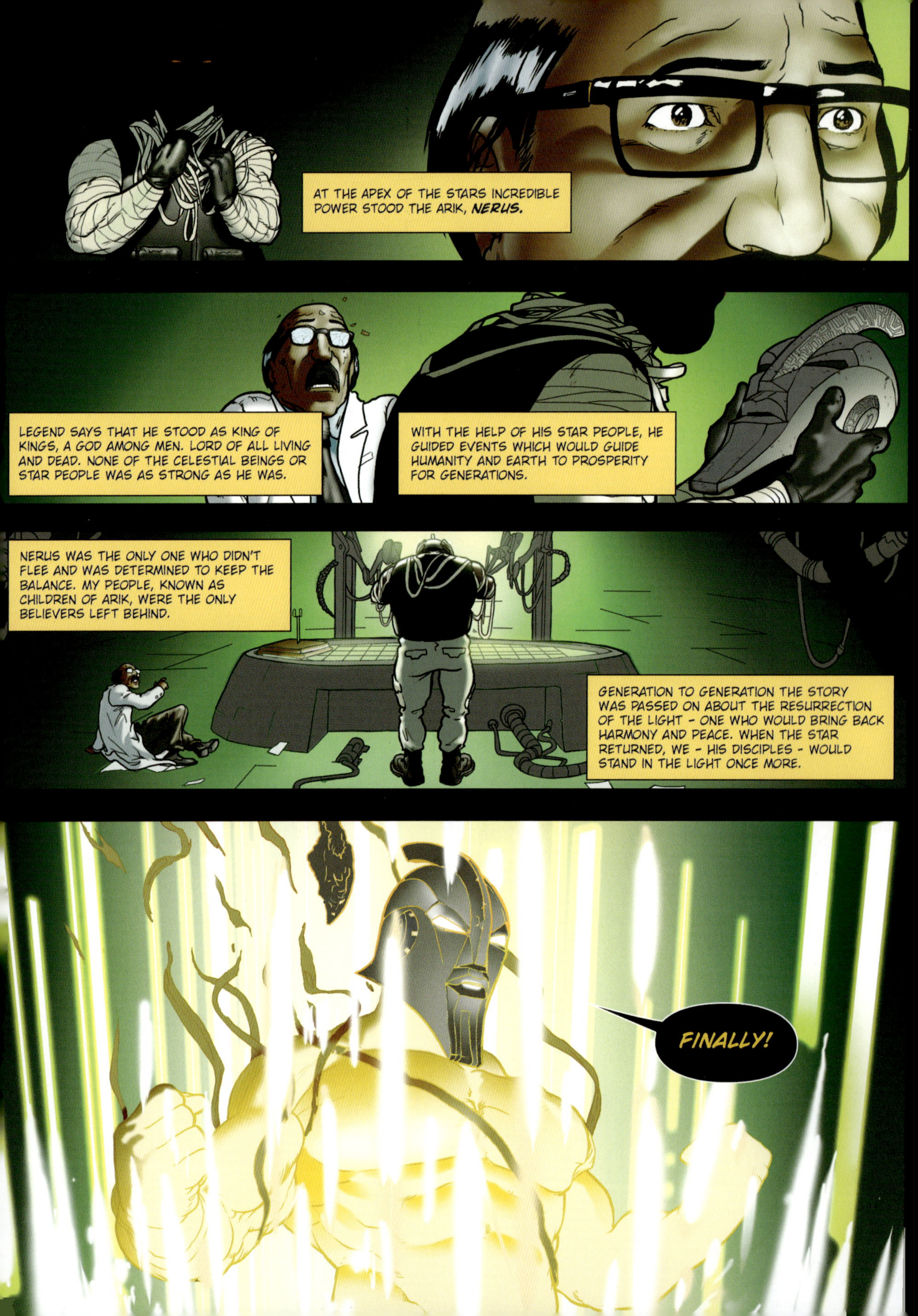

AT THE APEX OF THE STARS INCREDIBLE POWER STOOD THE ARIK, **NERUS.**

LEGEND SAYS THAT HE STOOD AS KING OF KINGS, A GOD AMONG MEN. LORD OF ALL LIVING AND DEAD. NONE OF THE CELESTIAL BEINGS OR STAR PEOPLE WAS AS STRONG AS HE WAS.

WITH THE HELP OF HIS STAR PEOPLE, HE GUIDED EVENTS WHICH WOULD GUIDE HUMANITY AND EARTH TO PROSPERITY FOR GENERATIONS.

NERUS WAS THE ONLY ONE WHO DIDN'T FLEE AND WAS DETERMINED TO KEEP THE BALANCE. MY PEOPLE, KNOWN AS CHILDREN OF ARIK, WERE THE ONLY BELIEVERS LEFT BEHIND.

GENERATION TO GENERATION THE STORY WAS PASSED ON ABOUT THE RESURRECTION OF THE LIGHT – ONE WHO WOULD BRING BACK HARMONY AND PEACE. WHEN THE STAR RETURNED, WE – HIS DISCIPLES – WOULD STAND IN THE LIGHT ONCE MORE.

FINALLY!